"Gus"

Our Incredible Resident Goose

by: Hazel Griffith

"Gus"

---Our Incredible Resident Goose

By: Hazel Griffith

Acknowledgements

I would like to give thanks to

my husband,
family members,
and friends

who gave constant encouragement to this endeavor.

Prologue

Welcome to our home!

Come observe the delightful pond and setting for our special family member. Meet Sox, our family cat, and view the pond from his chair, or walk along the brick path in the garden to the gate that opens to "The world of Gus".

There is a bench awaiting, a willow tree whispering an invitation, and some beautiful water lilies beckoning!

We want to share some of nature's beauty.

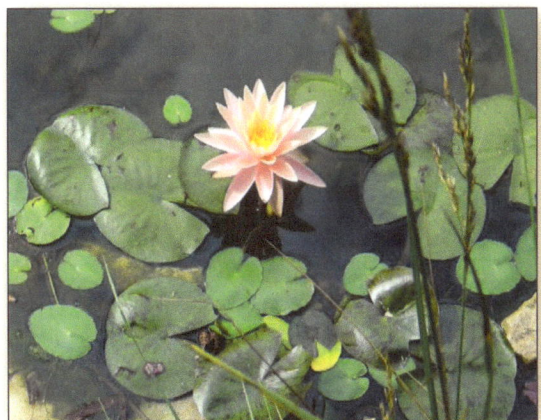

Chapter 1
Spring

It was spring and the wonders of the earth were on schedule. The grass was green, some bushes were in bloom, and colorful birds were dining at the six feeder smorgasbord. The pond (about an acre in size and 10-20 feet deep) showed much promise for the season. The pond depth had hidden many lively creatures during a brutally cold and snowy winter. Fish were once again showing their colors on the water's surface. Iris and other plants were popping up along the pond edge. Mallards and Wood Ducks were scouting the duck houses on the pond, while turtles crept upon the two wooden rafts to enjoy the warmth of the sun.

What is that? Oh, no…. the big Canada Geese are in the grass on the far side of the pond. If there are more than two we will chase them away. They leave droppings that are messy and not to our liking. John got out his paint ball gun (he would never harm them) and started down to the pond.

There was just one pair of geese and they were quickly aware of John's presence. When the resting goose stood up…. out popped SIX babies! Where had they had their nest with all the eggs? The babies must have been hatched nearby. We walk the pond daily. How could we have been unaware of their presence? There are so many and they are so lively! SO little and cute! These yellow-brown, fuzzy balls of energy are delightful!

Of course, John stopped and returned to the house. We would accept this new family until they left the pond. In years past it had usually only taken about four days for the parents to teach the babies the basics - how to swim, drink from the pond, eat grass, and even go under water to find tender morsels. It has been such fun to watch the protective parents teaching their family. And, it was amazing to see all six babies hide under Mom.

She just seemed to grow more fluffy as she covered her brood.

After only four days most goose families in the past had taken the family down the stream behind the pond to a body of water about a mile away. We could understand this action since we had a red fox family in the nearby meadow. One year we had seen a fox successfully snatch a baby from a brood. It was a sad experience to see…but nature has many creatures that need to be fed… cruel as it may seem.

Chapter 2
Help needed

This family seemed on schedule with their teaching and the babies were very active, as were the parents. We enjoyed their time with us and almost dreaded their departure though we knew it to be inevitable.

The fourth morning when John walked the pond he discovered an unbelievable scene!

There were no adult geese, but there were three very tiny, frightened baby geese on the grass at the pond edge. The poor babies had been abandoned! How can we provide shelter for them? The whole family had spent nights on a raft, safe from the fox. How could we be certain they would do the same. How would we keep them fed?

We called a woman known to work with abandoned wild fowl. She made a number of suggestions…

- do not approach the babies causing them to spend a lot of time in the water. They could drown. They have fuzz, not feathers with oil to make them water repellent.

- do not put up a house or safety structure. They will shy away from anything "new".

- do get duck food to supplement the natural food around the pond.

With great concern we followed her suggestions. Our row boat had been on shore all
the while, so John turned it up-side-down and put a brick under one end. They could use that
as a shelter. The two benches that we had on the shore were put together with the backs as a roof
and boards were added to keep out the rain. A food dish was added. All of this was very close to the
water edge. OK MR.FOX…we are trying to outsmart you!! The funny part was that they didn't
use any of these except the food dish. At night they swam straight out to a raft and stayed there all
night.   SMART BABIES!! We worried when rain came down in torrents, but they seemed almost
unaffected and stayed on their safe spot!!

The three were rarely separated. One lead the way and the other two were right at his tail forming
a tight triangle. This was true of them whether they were in the water or on land. SO CUTE !! If they
were resting in the grass they each faced a different direction to keep all angles under surveillance.

John was quickly accepted as someone they could trust. They were happy goslings! However, as
nature would have it, one was missing about a week later. Then two more nights and there was only
ONE goose. Yes, Gus was the lone survivor. He followed John around like a puppy dog. Gus greeted
John when he came with food, walked around the pond with John, busied himself eating grass, and
stayed on the raft much of the time.

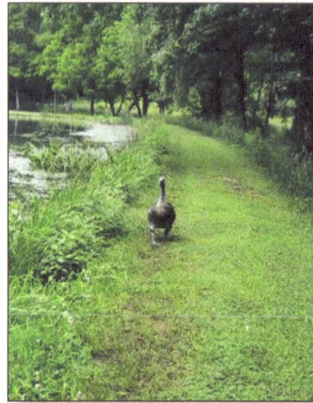

I was away for twelve days helping my sister move into a new home. The difference in Gus when I returned was amazing! He had been six weeks old when I left and nearly eight weeks old when I returned. He looked like a Canada Goose from a distance. Up close he still had lots of fuzz on his head, neck, and some on his body. He did have feathers, a tail, and the full Canada Goose coloring. His legs had looked like he was wearing wrinkled stockings and now the skin was filled out and taught. His feet were about 4 inches across and looked like soft black leather. Sometimes he stood with one foot partly covering the other! Funny! Why didn't he trip over his own feet?!

Chapter 3
Habits and learning

    Gus is a dear and so much fun! When we go down to the pond after dinner, he greets us with a nodding of his head and makes little high pitch noises. If we sit on the bench he lays at our feet and eats the tender grass around himself. Sometimes he falls asleep. Did you know that his eyelids are white and they come up from the bottom rather than from the top down? He may be asleep…but if you reach down to pet him he is suddenly awake and scoots out of reach.

    Sometimes we three walk the pond edge. Sometimes we run and he puts out his wings and runs with us.

Other times he walks with us and then slips into the water to swim along or swims across to where he knows we will soon be.

One day Gus had a dilemma. Three crows were heading for his food dish. Gus put his head down and charged at them. He acted angry. Then he backed away as if he were unsure. Did he really want to chase them away…or did he want to make friends?

When he is alone and seems a bit lonely, he plays on the pond. There are two gallon milk jugs anchored about fifteen feet apart that are his boxing bags. He hits them with his beak and then swims from one to the other.

Sometimes we see Gus in the water sitting very quietly in a small patch of water lilies. What a happy picture! And there are times when he eats the buds or blooms …just for fun!

Chapter 4
Time brings changes

The little sounds that Gus makes are very endearing. They are chirps and squeaks and sometimes he opens his mouth almost as if he is laughing. He has made a squawk but not a real "honk". When that happens, I think he will really be surprised!

It was a hot humid night when we went for our nightly walk (waddle) around the pond.

Gus didn't really want to walk that distance so he went into the water to swim along with us. John started to run and Gus wanted to keep up with him. Out went his wings and he "walked on water" to keep up with John. He is so near flight, but doesn't know about flying! It is so exciting to watch!

Did you know? …

- the life span of a Canada Goose is about 24 years
- their wing span is 4.2 to 5.6 feet
- their body measures 30 to 43 inches
- they weigh 6 to 19.8 pounds
- they can cover 1,500 miles in 24 hours
- they remain in a flock all year except when nesting
- they fly in a "V" formation to enhance their flying range
- when they drop out of formation they feel the drag of flying alone
- when the lead goose tires, it rotates in formation and another flies point
- if a goose is wounded or sick and drops out, another goose goes with him
   to stay with him until he dies or is able to fly.

Isn't it fun and amazing to learn about them?! Isn't he a handsome fellow?

Chapter 5
Changes

One day when I looked out the kitchen window to check on Gus....there was my ballet star standing on one foot and stretching one long wing, Great balance there Gus !

Another time he was our aquatic athlete. He was diving off the raft and disappearing under the water. Don't stay under so long Gus! Sometimes, his swims along with his head down in the water as if he were snorkeling. What's next?

Oh, Oh! There is a large blue Heron at the edge of the pond. He comes to fish in our pond. Gus is determined that this pond is his territory! Down goes his head and he charges the big Heron. Surprised, the Heron flew away. When the BIG snapping turtle came up to sun himself on a raft, Gus was not as ready to protect his domain. I can't blame him since snapping turtles have been known to harm ducks and geese.

Our baby has become a teenager. Most of the fuzz is gone, his voice chirps are now a deeper tone, and he has an "in charge" attitude.

John walked the pond one morning and as usual was greeted by Gus. However, his actions seemed strange. He would walk toward John and then away toward the pond. He did this a number of times. Each time he went closer to his food dish. Ah ha! He is now reminding John that he needs food. The deer have been eating his food again. And so…back to the garage for John to satisfy Gus's request.

When a friend visited we went to sit on a bench in the shade by the pond. We had hoped to visit with Gus. He was on a nearby raft and seemed reluctant to leave his solitary haven. With much coaxing he stood and flapped his big wings and stretched. Then, suddenly he was "walking on water" and heading straight toward us. He came to a halt like a bare foot water skier…heels down and large webbed feet as brakes! Our character!!

Then out came those large wings to impress us with his size and majesty as he came ashore.

One never really knows what to expect with Gus. One evening as we walked on the brick walkway in my flower garden and headed toward the pond, I spied a treat for Gus. It was a long earth worm. I scooped it up on a leaf and headed to the pond. We put the worm on top of his dry food like a cherry on a sundae. He was most intrigued! He cocked his head from side to side as he approached his dish. When he reached down for the worm it wiggled. HE JUMPED HIGH IN THE AIR! John and I couldn't stop laughing! Finally we had to remove the worm before Gus would return to his food. Imagine! I thought all birds liked worms!

We have tested Gus with all kinds of foods. Celery leaves are not really a treat. He loves to play with ice cubes on a hot summer night. He is selective with raspberries, they have to be dark and sweet. Watermelon is colorful and attracts his attention, but it is not very tasty. He often eats mint that grows on the pond edge. Tender new grass is a favorite.

Though Gus seems to be forever eating, he does take time to play with stones or leaves.

He finds shoe laces very interesting and puts a lot of effort into pulling them with all his might! The tip of a walking stick becomes a musical instrument when he rhythmically bites it!

Chapter 6
Learning to fly

The gradual steps toward learning to fly build a base for something that we take for granted…. birds flying. It starts with walking, then fast walking, and then walking with the help of their wings. Gus added swimming along with us as we walked. Then "walking on water" as we ran. When he lifted off the water it was very exciting! Then he practiced take-offs and landings, both from land and from water.

Days after we watched him practice, he surprised us with a full flight from one end of the pond to the other. When he landed it was as if he were laughing and saying," See, I can fly. I can really do it!"

When John went to feed Gus one morning he was at the far end of the pond. Rather than walking-on-water, he flew about ten feet above the water to John, circled John's head, and then flew back to the far end of the pond. A complete circle of flight! Upon landing in the water, Gus paddled back as quickly as his legs would carry him, looking like a very proud teenager. Gus likes routine as much as many humans and has repeated that flight for a number of mornings.

Like many of us, Gus plays many roles in his life with us. He is a guard of his territory.

When John fills the Hummingbird feeder, Gus is the supervisor and cleans up any spills.

When John added fresh soil to one area at the pond edge, Gus helped tamp it down to make it firm. When we take guests to the pond he is the official greeter with nods and squawks or wing flapping.

We are learning a great deal about geese and about our very special bird! There is still much to learn from Gus.

When you hear the term Canada Goose… What thoughts are conjured up in your mind? Do you think… big… beautiful… strong… mean… noisy… messy… frightening… majestic… distant… abundant?

After this time with Gus our understandings are considerably changed.

Big… yes, he likely weighs about 25 pounds and has a wing span of nearly 6 feet!

Beautiful… yes! God has given him distinctive markings and lovely subdued coloring.

Strong… maybe. But he certainly is not destructive.

Mean… not our Gus! But there are stories of people being chased by geese. Most likely the geese were guarding their nest or territory.

Noisy… as they fly they honk to encourage their leader. Gus is very quiet here on the ground.

Messy… when there are more than two they can produce an amazing amount of droppings.

Frightening… mostly "uncalled for" since they have size but do not have leg spikes like roosters or claws like some other large birds.

Majestic… very definitely! They have a regal appearance with dramatic coloring.

Distant… they travel in flocks and that is generally where their interest is shown.

Gus sometimes is distant with us and he does NOT allow us to touch him. How-ever, he looks for us, flies to us, and most often is interested in anything that we do.

Abundant… now-a-days more Canada geese winter over in the northern costal states.

The correct term is CANADA GEESE, not Canadian geese.

Would you be afraid of this "teddy bear" goose?

Chapter 7
Friends

Friends are so very important in our lives! Gus has shown how friendships can be developed with very unusual companions.

A mother deer and her speckled fawn came to the pond one early morning. Both Gus and the baby deer were very inquisitive about one another. They walked circles around each other while sizing-up the situation. The fawn started to frolic at the pond's edge and then ran about one-quarter way around the end of the pond. Gus joined the play and flew behind her! They were having fun together.

When a large blue heron came to the pond to fish for his dinner, Gus followed at a distance for nearly an hour. They acknowledged one another, but didn't really interact.

The big snapping turtle came up on the far raft to sun himself. Always vigil, Gus, swam   out to the raft and around it several times, but seemed to recognize the danger. He did not attempt to climb aboard!

One morning John looked and looked out the kitchen window. After much searching with binoculars, he got a glimpse of Gus in the tall grass of the meadow bordering the yard. Near Gus was a small fawn nestled in the deep grass. No adult deer was in view, but Gus had taken on the job of guarding the little one. He walked around the fawn a few times and then settled down very close to him. When the fawn got up and moved to a new spot, Gus followed quickly to be close to his charge. This went on for some time and finally the mother deer appeared. Gus turned his job over to the mother and the three of them wandered toward the pond and the dish of corn meant for Gus. It was time to share and relax.

And of course, human friends and acquaintances are interesting and fun! Our neighbor brought his 18 month old grandson to meet Gus. Gus loves children. They had great fun running together, and gentle Gus came just inches from his face for close scrutiny. Both enjoyed the sunshine and their time together. Two kids playing!

An indication of Gus wanting and needing company was obvious recently. John had left the main part of the back yard to work at the "holding pond" …the source of the water for the main pond. As he worked, John felt that someone was watching him. He turned to find Gus as his observer. Gus had crossed the entire back yard to seek out John's company. This could be a dangerous place for Gus because of the woods and high grass that could provide perfect hiding for the red fox. He was escorted back to the safer part of his domain.

Our property is unique in that we are down a long lane, and have a long sloping driveway with many trees. The back yard is an oval basin holding the acre pond and a like amount of grass area. Trees encircle it all! This is "The Domain of Gus" the Canada goose.

Chapter 8:
The "Maiden Flight".

Big, brave Gus has been flying around the back yard for some time now … but has not attempted to leave our property. He seems content to busy himself with friends right here at hand and within the confines of the tall bordering trees. We have been waiting for the day when he would leave the area. On a beautiful Sunday morning it happened!

As John opened the gate to take breakfast to Gus, the Blue Heron was frightened by this movement. The heron took off in flight and Gus right with him! Up and over the house and high trees they went! John stood in awe and disbelief. Was he gone forever … or an exciting excursion? We knew it would happen one day, but we weren't quite ready for his departure. John sat on the bench and waited. About five minutes later Gus came overhead and made a gliding landing onto HIS pond! I guess it was an excursion!

Since that "Maiden Flight" Gus has had a few such adventures. He does not seem any less satisfied with his home, and does seem majestic in his fulfillment of his role as ruler of the pond. He has been with us since his birth in late April and it is now September.

Every once in a while he greets John with a full compliment of all his flying tricks to impress us with his knowledge and maturity. It makes us smile, and even laugh aloud, as we recognize that he is an adult Canada Goose.

Chapter 9
Flights

Other geese have come to the pond and Gus has flown off with them, but he is back within minutes. However, he has been practicing his flying within the yard more and more. Straight flights are now giving way to circular flights and extended oval flights. Training flights!

One of the flights took on a laughable result when John and a guest were standing in the middle of the back yard looking at the house as they discussed some renovation plans. John had his back to the pond and was facing the man, when he saw the man's expression change to one of horror. The man said, "There is a BIG bird flying straight toward us!" … Gus landed at John's feet and was introduced!

Gus finds all kinds of friends to keep him company. When John looked out the window in the kitchen as he prepared his breakfast, he was privileged to observe a "Follow the leader" game made up of Gus and friends…. Gus, the Blue Heron, and two young deer all marching around the edge of the pond! Hollywood couldn't do it better!

Chapter 10
Winter approaches.

As winter chill sets in the pond has a covering glaze of ice. Gus thinks it is water and tries to push his chest through his usual routes. It does not work! What is this stuff?

He can not maneuver his body through the ice. Of course, he could lift-off and fly to his destination. He just seems puzzled and a bit frustrated.

In preparation for the colder and snowy weather we discuss some shelter possibilities. We know that we have been told that geese will not go to any new structure, but we are still determined to provide shelter for this dear creature. John is also aware that once the pond is frozen other animals do traverse the top. Fox, deer, dogs, etc. have all left their tracks in the past. We finally purchased a large, light weight, dog house and John mounted it on a sturdy metal frame structure a distance from shore. He even made a veranda on the front for Gus to sit on and for his feeding plate. We put foam and straw in the house. John put a container on the end of a long pole so that he could pour grain into his feeding plate while standing on shore. We thought we had done all we could and were satisfied with ourselves. However, to this day he has never gone into the house!! Yes, he has been on the veranda, but he likes, best of all, to swim up to the plate, eat a bit of grain, and then a drink of water as he swims. The squirrels, crows, and raccoons all enjoy The Gus Hotel!

When the ice first covered the pond Gus flew from the near end of the pond toward the farthest raft only to slide about 30 feet past his destination. He seemed confused but undaunted!

John and Gus have such an interesting relationship that it is fun to observe them together. As John installed the house (wearing wader boots) Gus was right there checking out every action. When John bent over to check a connection under water, Gus was right next to his face giving advice. I can't help but smile as I recall that day.

Now, if he would only see the benefit of the new house!

Chapter 11
Snow

Today was our first snow. The ice is snow covered. Gus can walk on the pond surface so much easier … but so can other animals. There are many fox tracks in view. We have seen two fox in the meadow behind our yard. When ever they come toward our yard we "bark" at them and chase them. They quickly run out of sight. Our hope is that they will realize that Gus has "family".

The white snow is beautiful but, like the down pouring of rain in the fall, it is something new for Gus to tolerate as an "outdoor" bird. He amazes me in that he does not seem in any way affected by either rain or snow. He sits quietly as the skies open up!

John makes sure that the ice is broken up near the influx of water. He also makes sure that Gus has a place to swim … in the frigid water …which he seems to love.

Deep snow can be a lonely time for one solitary goose. We watch him look for friends.

One morning he was on the near side of the pond on top of the overturned row boat beneath the pine trees. Upon closed examination of the scene, we located six deer sleeping in the snow under the pine trees.

Some days Gus walks along the far side of the pond and looks longingly toward the meadow where the deer come to graze in good weather and occasionally when there is snow.

One day recently Gus flew a strange mission, not above the tree tops, but under the tree branches. The deer were in the meadow and Gus was at the near end of the pond. He flew a large circle under the trees, above the deer, circled back under the trees, and ended at his starting point. It was an invitation to the deer to come to visit. Shortly after, the deer were all in our yard and Gus was in the center of the group.

Recently, John awakened in the night and decided to use a strong flashlight to check on Gus. Yes, there he was in the freezing water near his house. Two raccoon were in the house peering out at the light. He is sharing his house with new friends. Animals are so amazing!! They seem to sense each others needs, and care for their own as well.

Have you heard of Polar Bear Plunges for people? Have you ever taken part in one?

Gus has one daily!! And he seems to love it ! When he gets out of the water he flaps those large wings and struts around like he feels great! He is VERY special!

People ask … What is it like to have a pet Canada Goose?

First and foremost, he is not a" pet ". He is not confined in any way. His wings are NOT clipped, he is not caged, nor does he allow us to touch him. He could fly off at any time.

Our setting seems to be to his liking in any weather and so he has stayed with us these many months. Our bit of God's green acres is in a valley and down a long lane. Trees planted nearly thirty years ago tower at the end of our ranch house and a wooden board fence nearly obscures the pond when you drive down our sloping driveway. The back meadow has grown tall grasses, raspberry bushes, and wild flowers. This Canada Goose thinks it is his kingdom!

Chapter 12
Will winter never end?

It can't be…we are having spring like weather for a few days. John can't wait to clear the debris of winter from the pond edge!

With warm clothing and heavy gloves he sets out for the pond, tools in hand. And, of course, he is accompanied by Gus …the BIG helper.

Each time John raked some brown, dead growth from the pond, Gus was right there reaching down for the new, tender, green shoots. John was patient and tried to carefully place the rake without hurting his "helper". With smiles and happy cooperation the job progressed very slowly.

Winter came back with gusto but seemed more tolerable because of the sunshine and heavenly blue skies ….but at times it did seem never ending.

Finally more and more ice on the pond melted, giving Gus a larger swim area and increasing his safety from Mr. Red Fox. Others came to visit Gus.   Some very friendly and eager to share his pond and food. Two Hooded Merganser ducks came to dive under the water, feed, and entertain us. They are so colorful, lively, and pretty! They are like little fat corks bobbing in the water. Gus seemed to enjoy their presence. Various numbers of Canada Geese visited but they were bent on "owning " the pond and were mean to Gus. They chased him and bit at him. He is so gentle and has not learned to fight back. He retreated to far corners of the yard. We felt concerned for his safety. They were very persistent coming at night as well as daytime. John used his paint ball gun to chase them. The loud noise from the gun was quite effective. After using the gun a couple days and nights they did not return. Wood Ducks have had nests in our duck houses in past years, and they are among the happy visitors. They are colorful and interesting to watch. They had a fun game going this morning. Two distracted Gus while one ate from is food dish. Then they swam together and two different Wood Ducks did the distracting while another had his time at the food dish. They all swam together and gathered on a raft to rest. Gus seems content with their presence. Peace reigns.

Chapter 13:
Is our wish coming true?

As spring is advancing our hope for a mate for Gus is foremost. Just yesterday three geese came to the pond. Although the atmosphere seemed friendly, it was only a matter of moments before two started to taunt Gus. We were unhappy to realize that two were likely ones that had been here before, causing trouble. John dutifully went out with his paint ball gun. Again the sound scared them away. However, within about ten minutes one goose came back. She talked and talked to Gus. No advancement was made, but she kept chattering away. Gus turned his back on her. More chattering on her part, but silence from Gus. She seemed to really want to get to know him ….but the more she chattered the further he walked. Finally after about ten minutes she took to the air and did not return.

Although it is still early March there are many signs of spring to enjoy. The daffodils are up and have some buds, a few greens are showing in my flower garden, the poppy plant is already sizeable, and a daily variety of birds are at the large feeder. Like many other nature lovers, a new supply of plants and garden ornaments is being collected for the time they can be put in their homes out-of-doors. Spring is just around the corner!

During this slow advancement of spring a variety of ducks have been coming to keep Gus company on "his pond". The Wood Ducks are so pretty and they seem to enjoy the "Master" of the pond. The three seem to find much in common and spend hours in their various haunts on and around the pond. Two turtles were up on the rafts yesterday. Gus took a spin around each raft checking on the old friends from last fall.

One goose came to visit a number of times. Sometimes she came alone and other times with another pair of geese. The three stayed around a day or two. They seemed to enjoy our pond and food, but Gus always seemed to stay off to the side of the group.

Then one night they all (Gus included) flew off over the trees. The next day the pair returned… but not Gus ! Was it a final departure? Actually, no! The day and evening passed … but the next morning… there was Gus! I guess he will be with us a while longer. We are truly privileged !

It has been some time since Gus and I have had a conversation. The snow and slippery weather has kept me from pond visits during the winter. Recently, when the weather was a bit warmer, I could not resist the opportunity to walk in my flower garden to survey the needs of spring. Gus was quick to spot me and make himself known with deep honks! And so, the gate was flung open and I clapped my hands, while calling his name. His wings went wide and he waddled hurriedly up the steep incline to the gate. I bowed and he bowed, we talked about how happy we were to see each other, and his bill came just inches from my face! What a wonderful greeting of two friends ! Gus followed me into the garden and tasted a few of the fresh green weeds. Pulling a few weeds and tossing them to Gus kept our conversation going for a while. He seems to feel it a privilege to come into may garden and only stayed for a few minutes before going back to "his" domain. With the gate still open wide he stood and observed. That called for another close conversation before closing the gate. He is such a dear!

Chapter 14:
Spring treasures.

Each day of spring brings new treasures. All we have to do is look for them!

Geese are now visiting often and they are friendly to Gus. Three visited recently and spent the entire day swimming, eating, and relaxing with Gus. How great is nature? Shortly after that day, a single goose came visiting and they did seem to enjoy each others company. Late that afternoon she flew away. How tantalizing for us who desire a mate for our guy.

Each day there is a variety of pond visitors. The Hooded Mergansers are back, along with the Wood Ducks, and Herons. To add to the beauty the colorful Koi are now visible in the water and the daffodils are full and colorful. All this, seen from our kitchen windows.

At night the raccoons can be seen at the "Gus Hotel". They are like cute little old men ambling about, squinting at our flashlight.

The deer come to feed in the meadow and they are a delight for Gus. He invites them to our yard and his food dish. If they resist his offer, he goes to the meadow to join them.

It seems that they look after him when the red fox is in the neighborhood.

Human friends come to visit as well! A friend had built a tall sailboat that was run by remote control. He brought his two grandchildren with him to try the boat out on the pond.. What a beautiful sailboat! Gus was very curious and came to see for himself. How fascinating! Once the boat was put into the water, Gus swam close behind. What fun! This was something so new and unusual. It all went well until the boat turned and headed back with Gus feeling like a target. He was not very pleased and quickly made his way to one side and then happily resume his trailing activity.

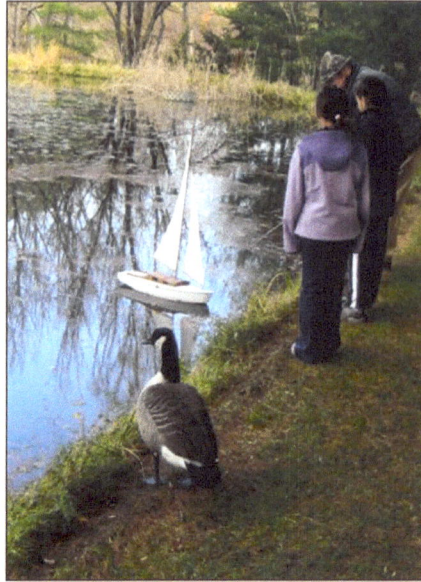

Chapter 15:
New adventures.

Our fears for the safety of Gus are beginning to seem unwarranted. He is a very large goose and has established himself as "ruler of his pond". A mature red fox was in the yard headed for Gus when he honked loudly causing the fox to retreat. We were happily surprised! John added his loud commands to Gus's honks.

Although Gus has joined me in my flower garden, he has not ventured into the front yard.
However, recently he had not only gone into the front yard, but up the driveway and part way up the lane to a neighbors yard. John discovered him as he walked up the lane to get the mail from our mailbox. They returned happily to the back yard and to "The Gus Domain".

When we got tornado warnings (unheard of here in Maryland) we were concerned for Gus. The rain was so heavy and the wind so strong that we could hardly identify Gus on his raft. He stood his ground on his "safe" raft and made it through the storm looking as
handsome as ever!   Amazing !

Recently, when we had guests visiting and went to the pond to talk with Gus, our guest used her I-Pod to play geese sounds. It was so interesting to observe Gus as he cocked his head and tried to find the geese making the sounds. Were they coming in for a landing, or
hidden behind the trees, or somewhere out of sight? Yes, our Gus has even been exposed to modern technology… but he is still our wild friend.

Chapter 16
Adventures abound

One of the spring activities is often the use of the row boat to check the water inlet, drain, and duck houses on the pond. John enjoyed the company of his pond supervisor, Gus. As the boat went from place to place Gus followed close behind. Then it was time for some fun! John rowed toward Gus! He was undaunted and took the game in stride! He does trust his buddy!

John also lowered the water level to make pond edge work a bit easier. That lead to another game! The colorful Koi fish swam in the more shallow water near The Gus Hotel. When Gus swam above them his feet actually touched the Koi. They both seemed to think this was a game. Animal life is often trusting and always interesting!

Chapter 17
A natural process

Our close contacts with Gus have revealed to us a natural process in the lives of geese. There is a season each year when they molt. What is molting? It is a process whereby geese lose some of their feathers. Many were found around the pond. Some seem to drop out while others are pulled out by him. At the present Gus has lost his flight feathers and can not fly. When he stretches out those big wings they look very strange and small for his large frame.

He does not attempt to fly. It will take a few weeks for the feathers to be replaced. In the meantime Gus seems content to rest in the grass under the shade of trees by the pond. Life goes on.

As I walk in my garden each day Gus comes up to the outside of the wooden fence to talk with me and looks forward to some "sweet treats". I pull up weeds, clover, and even some of the prolific sweet Alyssum to share with him. Special treats are always important, especially when he can not fly!

Just last night when I checked the back yard, Gus was stretching his wings and looking a bit lonely. His neck was stretched and his head was high, as if looking for some friends.

That was a cue for me to go out to see him. I gathered some "sweet weeds" and opened the gate. Gus put his head down and came rushing to me … as if to say "Oh, I am so happy to see you. I just want to get to you as fast as I can!" What a very special greeting!

Some gentle honks and muted sounds came from his throat to acknowledge my gifts and presence.

Chapter 18.
We are so BLESSED !

Who could ask for more? We are enjoying our 30th year here in this heavenly place. We feel that nature has kept us grounded and we are grateful for our special relationship with some of God's creatures.   Gus has been a very unique acquaintance and may be with us for his lifetime. Only God knows the plan. God is good!

www.ingramcontent.com/pod-product-compliance
Lightning Source LLC
Chambersburg PA
CBHW060819270326
41930CB00002B/86